A Book of Praises and Prayers

Caroline Parkinson

Presentation by *BookLeaf Publishing*

Web: www.bookleafpub.com

E-mail: info@bookleafpub.com

ISBN: 9789395223508

First edition 2022

ACKNOWLEDGEMENT

This book would not exist without the sovereign hand of God. May all glory, honor, praise, and thanksgiving be to Him forever and ever!

1.

How many are your wondrous works toward me,
O God of my righteousness!
They are beyond count.
When my soul is weary, your promises are my
strength;
when I am cast down, your praises bear me up.

The enemy crushes my life to the gound and my
sin surrounds me,
but you, O Lord, come to fight for me;
you do not leave me alone.

Who can stand against you, Speaker of creation?
Though my strength fails and I fall,
your mercy holds me; it has no limit.

Let me remember in the day of my trial to seek
your face,
O Lover of my soul,
for you alone are my refuge, my kinsman
Redeemer.

2.

Why are you silent, O my soul?
Why do you not sing with your brothers?
Lift up your voice and give thanks!
Make a joyful noise,
for your name is written in the Lamb's Book of
Life;
it is written in blood, and none can erase it.

Why are you silent, O my soul?
Why do you not mourn with your sisters?
Lift up your voice in weeping for those lost in
darkness.
Cry warning to those who are perishing.
Make known to them the Way of salvation;
proclaim to all peoples the Lamb that was slain.

Why do you clamour, O my soul?
Why do you rush to and fro, as if your ability is
your own?
Cease your crying and be silent.
Put to death your fretting and be still,
for the Lion of Judah is the One who fights for
you.
Who can stand against the fierce might of his
love?

And what can turn away his thoughts toward
you?
I will hope in my Beloved and I will set my gaze
upon him,
Then will my soul be still, and I shall lie down
in peace.

3.

What is this sorrow, O my soul?
Lay down this longing that steals your days.
What do you search for among the sons of men?
It is already found in the Beloved.

Why do you weep, O my soul?
What is this sorrow that has darkened your eyes?
Lift your face and see: your Redeemer is at
hand.
He does not despise your tears,
nor will he turn away his face from you.
He carries your sorrow in his hands and his feet,
your comfort is poured out from his side.
Lift up your eyes and see, for he is doing a new
thing.
He is planting a seed in you,
and in his fullness of time will you reap its
harvest.
Trust in the Lord

4.

Great is your name, O God Almighty,
and greatly to be praised.
You breathe on the waters, and the hurricane is
put to shame.
When the sole of your foot touches the ground,
the whole earth heaves in exultation.
All of nature quivers at the sound of your voice;
it is undone for joy at your presence.

Your name is my covering, O Lord my God.
When cares overwhelm me,
when desires oppress me,
when my soul is tempted to despair,
I run to your name, and I am safe.
I sing praise to your name,
and you refresh my soul.
O holy One, my Friend and my Beloved,
put your song in my heart,
and let your praises be ever on my lips.

5.

How blessed is your providence, O Lord
Almighty!
How steadfast your wisdom to guide our paths!
What shall we fear when held in your hand?
Shall we fear loneliness or pain? Hunger or
death?
We shall fear you alone, O God, and terror will
flee from us.
In reverence and awe we will worship your
name;
with joy we will extol your grace!
In power and mercy you have cast down death;
in wisdom you have broken every chain!
How blessed is your love, O God our Father!

6.

What shall we desire beyond you, O God?
In Heaven and Earth there is none like you,
strong in mercy, joyful to save,
abounding in steadfast love.
By your grace you have filled our souls.
We have tasted your goodness,
and nothing else shall satisfy.
Teach us your ways, Father of lights;
on level paths guide our feet to the Fountain of
Life,
that we may drink deeply of your love,
and find perfect satisfaction in your heart.

7.

8

How wondrous is your salvation, O Lord our
God;
it is too wondrous for the mind to fathom!
How abundant is your grace and your mercy;
the heart cannot contain them!
We were far off, foreigners and enemies,
strangers to your name and hostile to your ways.
Yet in mercy you pierced our hearts,
your steadfast love has scattered our darkness
and given us Light.
You have given Life for Death.
With humility we will praise your name!
In joy we will offer thanks to you, and sing of
your salvation!

8.

Look to the Lord, all you who are crushed,
taste and see what a wondrous salvation he has
worked for us!
If I ascend to the highest heavens, it soars far
beyond.
If I sink into the deeps of the deep, it descends
futher still.
To the fathest corners of the dark it finds me
and carries me to the the Rock, my Refuge.
Despair is cast out and peace reigns in its stead.
He consumes my rags in his holy fire
and clothes me in his shining righteousness.
Take heart, you who lie in the dust.
See the One who was pierced,
and behold how great a price he himself has
payed.
It was not in vain, but for his namesake
he who paid so dearly will surely gather all he
has bought.
O that I might see my Redeemer!
May all my love be poured out for him who
poured out all for me,
that I might dwell in his presence forever.
O Lord, hear!

9.

What shall satisfy our souls?
Wealth is dead, it cannot save.
Our love is fleeting,
when darkness comes, will it stay?
As for life, it lingers for a moment
and passes away,
swallowed up and forgotten
in the blink of an eye.
Where can we turn?
We will turn to you, O God,
our Living Treasure!
You alone are mighty to save;
O redeem us from this body of death!
Only your love is steadfast and true.
Give us of your love,
that we would be beacons in the darkness,
guiding wayward souls to you.
You, our Lord, are Life eternal;
apart from you is only death.
When all has faded and passed away,
you remain.
Be the Life that is in us, Holy One,
and let our dwelling be with you
for all eternity!

10.

My Beloved is mighty and fierce.
In carelessness I wandered from His presence,
and was caught in a snare.
I cried out in anguish
"Oh that I had held fast to the Beloved!"
and He heard.
See, He has rent the Heavens;
He comes bounding over the mountains to save
me,
He crosses the seas in a stride
and my enemies flee before His passion.
What sweet relief when He lifts me in His arms;
how tenderly He cradles me to His heart!
With His hands He cleanses my wounds
and binds them up;
His tears wash my face.
He carries me rejoicing to the place of His
dwelling
and covers me in His riches.
My heart bursts with the goodness
of the One who loves my soul.
Oh my God, my Beloved,
that I might be faithful as you are faithful!

11.

What need I but you?
And what shall I desire beyond you?
You are the One I adore, O God,
The Lover of my soul.
The love of man is but a vapor,
it cannot be grasped or held.
Earthly comfort is like the wind,
who knows which way it will blow?
Your love, O Lord, is steadfast and sure.
Laying hold of its own, it does not let us go.
Though our strength fails, your grip never
weakens.
As a tree sends its roots into the heart of a
mighty mountain,
and is not moved,
so will I put my hope and trust in your eternal
Love,
and you, O mighty One, will keep my hope
secure.
My song is to you, my Father and my King,
for all of your wondrous works toward me,
the half of which you have not even begun to
pour out.
My song is to you, my Lord and my God,
for you alone are worthy.

You are all in all, and there is none like you.
O my God, may my soul praise you with
thanksgiving forever,
and my my lips never cease to bless your holy
name!

12.

How steadfast is the love of the Lord!
The dawn declares His patience and grace,
and the night is filled with His promises.
Who is faithful like our God?
Who can match His unwavering rhythm?

Let my heart praise you, O Lord!
In all my affliction, you are the answer;
who else is there to satisy?
I call to mind your tender mercies
and my soul worships you,
for you alone are worthy.
How can I keep silent?
May my lips hurry to recount your marvelous
deeds!
For though my feet stumble, you carry me.
Though my eyes wander, you come to me and
lead me back.
Though me heart grows cold, the flame of your
love
is ever burning; you rekindle my affections.

Sing to the Lord, all you his people!
Sing His praise, O my soul!
For His mercy is unceasing,

and His grace is to all nations.
How steadfast is the love of the Lord!

15

13.

Your presence, O God, is a refining fire;
wickedness is consumed by your gaze.
If I regard evil in my heart, I shall perish with it.
O God, consume my arm, that my soul may live!
Have mercy on me, a faithless and wicked
servant,
and sift out the evil that is in my heart for your
namesake.
It is better to pass through the Refiner's fire,
than in comfort to sink into Gehenna.
I will wait for you, my gracious Father,
until you are done your work.
I will wait for you until your salvation is
complete,
and I will offer up praise with my lips.
I will sing to you, my God and Father;
my heart will sing!
Praise the Lord, you who have known His
salvation;
sing songs of His mercy!
Exalt the grace of our Redeemer;
ascribe power to His name.
O bless the Lord forever!

14.

Oh God, you have been my refuge,
leave me not naked on the rock!
The enemy is full of fury;
my path is full of snares,
and his arrows find me in the dark.
Shield me in the cleft,
that the waves would not break over me!
Hide me in your shadow and go before me,
that my foot might not stumble.
In your righteousness I am clothed;
your purity is my covering,
and your grace my shield.
Surely, surely you will deliver.
Though my soul be bowed down to the dust,
you will not permit me to be dragged to Sheol;
you will deliver.

Oh that my gratitude would rise to you before all
men!
May my soul declare your excellence,
and may my lips tell of your salvation!
From your mouth justice goes forth,
and mercy springs from your heart.
Blessed be God my refuge!

15.

Be still, my soul.
Cease your clamour.
Wait on your God.
For the battle is the Lord's;
He will fight.
Trust not in strength.
Hope not in plans.
The Lord of armies heeds not your plans,
and by what is weak He puts strength to shame.
Send the singers to the front!
The choir shall be the first
to stand against the enemy,
for my weapons are not made of steel,
nor are they fashioned by human hands,
but my weapons flash forth from my heart,
they pour from my lips.
They are songs of praise to my God.
The Lord of hosts has chosen them for me.
Oh my King, ride out victoriously
for the cause of your servant,
that your name would be hallowed.
Will you abandon your children?
Your tender ones will die without your
presencce.
Shall those who bear your name be defensless?

May you guard your name jealously!
For merciful and gracious is your name.
Deliverance belongs to the Lord;
He knows the time for grief
and the time for salvation.
Truly, truly though grief
He purchased our salvation,
and laid down His own life
that we might take it up.
Do not fear, my soul,
take up your song!
Make a joyful noise,
and behold the salvation
that the Lord will accomplish.
Praise the Lord of hosts!

16.

The Lord, the Lord is God, and there is no other.
Whose wisdom will guide us when the way is
veiled?
The eyes of the Lord pierce deepest night;
they are on His beloved ones even through the
valley of death.
Do you regard darkness, O Lord?
Your eyes are a flame of fire; the light of your
gaze scatters every cloud.
What path is there that you have not known,
mighty God?
In faithfulness you have set my feet in this way,
that I might learn discipline.

My soul is in anguish day and night, and my
spirit lies broken within me,
yet in this I hope, and because of this my joy is
alive:
your loving kindness has chosen this path for me
to lead me to your streams of grace;
your mercy upholds me, that I might not fall
headlong.
The road is treacherous and full of pitfalls;

when I watch them they grow in number and I
cannot escape them.
I will set my gaze on the radiance of your face,
and you will set my feet on solid ground.

You are all my hope, O God! My life is in you.
Do not let my heart despair what has been lost in
this life,
for it passes like a breath and is gone.
Set my heart on what is eternal.
You are eternal!

Who can search out your wisdom, O Lord?
For it reaches beyond the heavens.
Who is there to question you?
Who will say to you "it should have been thus"?
With you there are no mistakes; you do all
things well.
Blessed is the one who walks the path that you
set before them,
for all your ways lead to life.
Lead on, my Lord and my God!

17.

Blessed are those who fear the Lord,
for they turn aside from the follies of death
to seek the way of Life.
Blessed are they who trust in His goodness,
for to know that He exists is well,
but to know that He is good brings life!

In all our mourning we are blessed,
for the Lord Himself is our Comforter.
In all our trials we are blessed,
for the Father of mercies is our reward.

Call on Him in the day of trouble,
and He will hear.
He does not hear with the ears of man,
with puffed up pride and selfish ambition,
but He hears with the heart of the gentle and
lowly Savior,
desiring that all might reach repentance.
Will He not lead you in the way of salvation?

He guards His namesake jealously.
Will He not then also keep those who bear His
name?

Trust in the Lord, and you will not be put to shame.

18.

Call on the name of the Lord, all you who would
be saved!
Why do you seek life among what is dead?
Shall fleeting pleasures sustain you?
Can passing delights save your soul?
Behold, they are the very instruments of death!
Through their treacherous caress many are lured
to destruction.

Who can save but our God?
Who can impart life but Life Himself?
Jesus is His name!
His pardon is promised to all who confess,
for all men are born into death,
and none has the power to escape its bondage.
Who is the man who will ransom his friends?
Though he were given a thousand lifetimes,
he could not even pay for his own soul.

Behold the holy God!
He has tasted our every weakness and has
prevailed over them all.
The living God conquered death by death,
and the slain Lamb is alive forevermore!
Behold the Ransom for your soul!

Oh lay down your wicked and fleeting pleasures,
and take up the joy incorruptible!
See how beautiful is the face of Him who loves
your soul;
it is radiant with the glory of His love!

How tenderly He walks with me, and His
fellowship is my delight.
Those who love Him lack no good thing, for He
is all in all.

Fall upon His mercy and repent, and He will
show you faithfulness,
for in Him every promise is yes and amen!
Oh believe in the beautiful name of Jesus Christ!